Dedication

This book is dedicated to the great God almighty, also to my fiancé, Sinque Morrison and my children.

Jeremiah 29:11 For I know the thoughts that I think toward you, saith the Lord, thoughts of peace, and not of evil, to give you an expected end.

Proverbs 3:5-6 Trust in the Lord with all thine heart; and lean not unto thine own understanding.

6 In all thy ways acknowledge Him, and He shall direct thy paths.

Joshua 1:9 Have not I commanded thee? Be strong and of a good courage; be not afraid, neither be thou dismayed: for the Lord thy God is with thee whithersoever thou goest.

Hebrews 13:8 Jesus Christ the same yesterday, and to day, and for ever.

Hebrews 4:16 Let us therefore come boldly unto the throne of grace, that we may obtain mercy, and find grace to help in time of need.

Psalm 18:33 He maketh my feet like hinds' feet, and setteth me upon my high places.

salm 91:15-16 He shall call upon me, and I will answer him: I will be with him in trouble; I will deliver him, and honour him.

16 With long life will I satisfy him, and shew him my salvation.

Psalm 28:7 KJV

The Lord is my strength and my shield; my heart trusted in him, and I am helped: Therefore my heart greatly rejoiceth; and with my song will I praise him.

Exodus 15:2 The Lord is my strength and song, and he is become my salvation: he is my God, and I will prepare him an habitation; my father's God, and I will exalt him.

1 Corinthians 16:13 Watch, stand fast in the faith, be brave, be strong.

Isaiah 50:9 Behold, the Lord God will help me; who is he that shall condemn me? lo, they all shall wax old as a garment; the moth shall eat them up.

Isaiah 43:19 Behold, I will do a new thing; now it shall spring forth; shall ye not know it? I will even make a way in the wilderness, and rivers in the desert.

Micah 7:7-8 Therefore I will look unto the Lord; I will wait for the God of my salvation: my God will hear me.

Rejoice not against me, O mine enemy: when I fall, I shall arise; when I sit in darkness, the Lord shall be a light unto me.

Isaiah 45:5 I am the Lord, and there is no other;
apart from me there is no God.
I will strengthen you.

John 14:1-4 Let not your heart be troubled: ye believe in God, believe also in me.

2 In my Father's house are many mansions: if it were not so, I would have told you. I go to prepare a place for you.

3 And if I go and prepare a place for you, I will come again, and receive you unto myself; that where I am, there ye may be also.

Isaiah 41:10 So do not fear, for I am with you;
do not be dismayed, for I am your God.
I will strengthen you and help you;
I will uphold you with my righteous right hand.

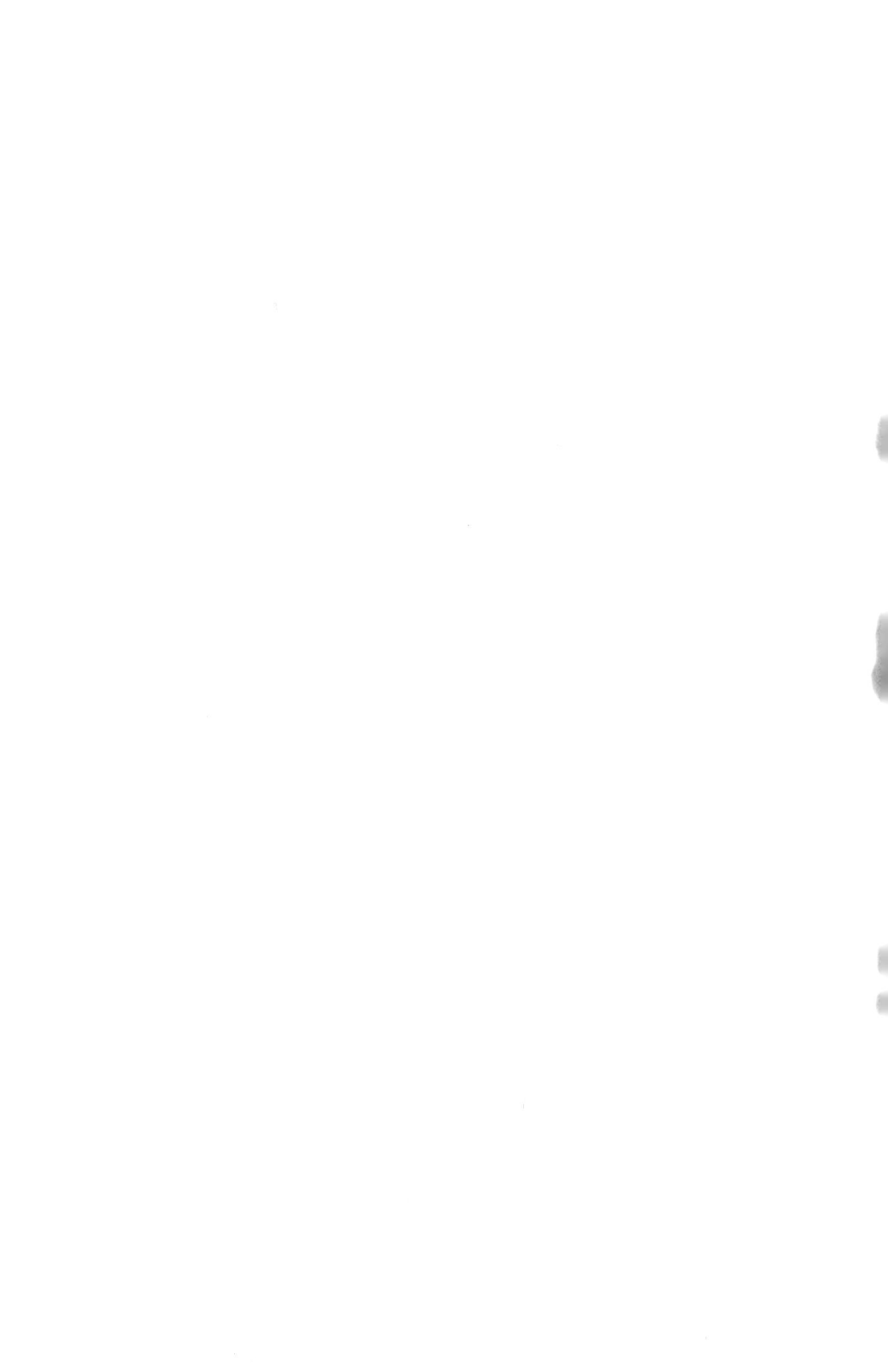